The Wonder of a Love

A letter from Brother Roger of Taizé

GEOFFREY
CHAPMAN
MOWBRAY

WJK

Introduction

It is now forty years since young adults started flocking in ever greater numbers to the little French village of Taizé. Brother Roger had arrived there in 1940 to begin a monastic community. Today, at certain points during the summer, the young people can number up to six thousand a week, coming from as many as seventy different countries at one time. Taizé's founder writes:

'If the faith had not been so shaken in many parts of the world, our community would not be committing so much energy to welcoming young people, week after week, all through the year, not only from north, south and eastern Europe, but also Africans, North and South Americans and Asians. Many of them are searching for a meaning to their lives. The question, "What does God expect of me?" keeps coming up. What my brothers and I would like to be for them is men who pray and who listen, never spiritual masters.'

It is to support the young in their search that Taizé launched a 'pilgrimage of trust on earth'. Far from organizing a movement around the Community, this pilgrimage encourages the young to be creators of peace and bearers of reconciliation in their own cities and villages and in their parishes, with all generations, from children to the elderly.

At the end of every year, a new stage in the pilgrimage is marked by the 'European meeting for young adults' which Taizé prepares and which can bring together as many as 100,000 people from east and west. They spend five days together in a major city such as Prague, Rome, London, Budapest, Munich, Vienna or Paris.

During each of these meetings, Brother Roger publishes an open letter which he has been preparing throughout the preceding year. 'The Wonder of a Love' is one of these letters. It has been translated into sixty languages, including twenty-one Asian and nine African.

Beyond the European meeting itself,

these yearly letters reach young people across the whole of Europe and other continents too. They accompany gatherings of the 'pilgrimage of trust' in India, in the Philippines, in South Africa, in North America . . . All through the year in Taizé, they provide the basic themes of meditation for everyone taking part in the intercontinental meetings there.

Today, through this little book, 'the wonder of a love' is being offered to all those, young and old alike, who want to build their lives around a few simple realities of the Gospel.

Christ of all compassion, we thirst to hear you tell us: 'Rise up, may your soul live!' We never wish to choose darkness or discouragement but to welcome the brightness of your presence: it sustains us, it inspires us.

Jesus our joy, when we understand that you love us, something in our life is pacified and even transformed. We ask you: 'What are you expecting of me?' And we know that you always reply: 'Let nothing trouble you, I am praying within you, dare to give your life.'

The wonder of a love

By night, we will go to the spring. Deep within us there sparkles living water where we can quench our thirsts.

By night and by day, as we move forward from beginning to new beginning, a whole life is built up.

Could the human soul be that, too: the secret heartbeat of a happiness almost beyond words?

In the presence of physical violence or moral torture a question plagues us: if God is love, where does evil come from?

No one can explain the why of evil. In the Gospel, Christ enters into solidarity with the incomprehensible suffering of the innocent; he weeps at the death of someone he loves.[1]

Did not Christ come to earth so that every human being might know that he or she is loved?[2]

When we can sense hardly anything of God's presence, what good is it to agonize over it?

----

[1] John 11.35–36

[2] 'There is no violence in God. God sent Christ not to accuse us, but to call us to himself, not to judge us, but because he loves us.' (Letter to Diognetus, second century after Christ.) There are physical forms of violence on earth: war, torture, murder . . . There are other forms of violence too; those that are concealed in the ploys of mistrust and of cunning, in suspicion, humiliation, an unkept promise . . .

Having the desire to welcome God's love is enough for a flame to be kindled little by little in the secret recesses of our being. 'Filled by his love, the heart opens to others.'[3]

Animated by the Holy Spirit, this flame of love may be quite fragile. Yet it keeps burning.

The Holy Spirit stirs us up and is at work within us, reorientating the depths of our being,[4] preparing us to live lives of forgiveness and reconciliation.

. . . And the heart awakens to the wonder of a love.

[3] An Orthodox theologian from Bucharest, Father Staniloae, who died in 1993, and who had been in prison for his beliefs, wrote words so essential that we would like to know them by heart: 'I looked for God in the human beings of my village, then in books and in ideas. But that brought me neither peace nor love. One day, while reading the Church Fathers, I discovered that it was possible to encounter God through prayer. I gradually realized that God was close to me, that he loved me, and that filled by his love, my heart opened to others. I realized that love was a communion, with God and with others. And without that communion, everything is only sadness and desolation.'

[4] In the depths of our being, a little part of ourselves remains solid, unshakeable as rock.

In a breath of silence

To allow ourselves to be refreshed by living water welling up within us, it is good to go off for a few days in silence and peace.

In ancient times Elijah, the believer, set out in search of a place to listen to God. And there he made this discovery: God's voice finds a way of making itself understood in a breath of silence.[5]

God is familiar with our longings. He perceives better than we do our most basic intentions and what lies deep within us. What we have trouble grasping in prayer, God has already understood.

When we pray and nothing seems to happen, does our prayer remain unanswered? No. The fire of love penetrates even the arid regions, even the contradictions, of our being.

In quiet trust in God all prayer finds some kind of fulfillment. Perhaps it is different than we expected … Does not God answer us with a view to a greater love?[6]

The beauty of prayer with others is an incomparable support. Through simple words and symbols it communicates a discreet and silent joy.

---

[5] I Kings 19.3–13.

[6] Happy those who live in trust of heart; they will see God! How will they see him? Like Mary who, attentive, 'kept everything in her heart' (Luke 2.19,51) and saw God with her inward eye. A vision can be given by the Holy Spirit. But it is not the appearance of a person, known or unknown, who stands alongside us. It is an image drawn from within ourselves, clear enough to allow us to 'see' a loved or venerated being. It is possible to love Christ so much that we have such a vision, brought into being by the Holy Spirit. But what are visions or ecstasies when compared to an act of love, of forgiveness, of reconciliation?

A breeze of trusting

Who will find ways of preparing and opening up children and young people to the mystery of trust in Christ?[7] Glimpsed in the early years, an intuition of faith develops in a person's heart of hearts and even if it is forgotten, it can reappear throughout his or her life.[8]

But why are some people seized by the wonder of a love and know that they are loved and even filled to overflowing? Why do others have the impression that they are neglected, not very much loved for what they are?[9]

[7] Take a child by the hand, go with that child into a church to pray . . . and he or she can be awakened to the mystery of faith. This is possible at home too. In the fourth century, Saint John Chrysostom wrote: 'The home is a little church.' Today, in secularized societies, it is good for our homes to provide glimpses of an invisible presence by means of a few symbols of Christ. We can set up a corner for prayer, however small, with an icon, a candle . . . Of course, making one's home a little church, an 'ecclesiola', should never mean becoming a closed group and thus forgetting the universal dimension of the Church.

[8] Faith can reappear in adulthood in people who have prayed with members of their family as children. However, when there is a void in childhood, this void is sometimes filled in whatever way possible, with elements that happen to come to hand. How could a child have the maturity to sort out these elements?

[9] As a result of different events, a child can experience feelings of rejection. And in that child an inner appeal is born not to be abandoned. Children are wounded by tensions in their family and by arguments which adults have in their presence. Understanding a child or a young person requires a great deal of discernment. The question often arises: 'Will someone be there to help them through the void that afflicts them deep within their hearts?

Every human being yearns to be loved as well as to love. It is not for nothing that the Gospel alerts us about not becoming locked up in isolation.

When we are listened to, obstacles fall away: frustrations of the heart; wounds from a recent or distant past. Being listened to is the beginning of a healing of the soul.[10]

And the breath of a trust arises . . . and a gateway to freedom begins to open up.

[10] Being listened to by someone of experience who can detect what lies beneath the contradictions of our being. Listening does not require a method, but knowing how to discern the gifts, the wounds and the thirst for God in those who come with something to confide. There are elderly people who are able to listen, to understand the young, and to unburden them of a load of worry.

A fathomless thirst for freedom

Although human beings are fragile, they have a fathomless thirst for freedom.

Like the most beautiful of coins, freedom can have another side. What kind of freedom would it be if, used in a self-centred way, it harmed the freedom of others? Freedom is intimately linked to forgiveness and reconciliation.[11]

Here too Christ invites us to a humble repentance. And what is repentance? It is a surge of trust by which we place our failings in him, surrendering ourselves to him in silence and in love.

[11] Even under the guise of loving someone, it is possible to keep them captive in a desert of emotional blackmail. Even in the name of freedom, it is possible to manipulate another person.

The humble trusting of faith

Jesus was a human being. He knows how humans aspire to inner peace. And before leaving those he loved, he assured them that they would receive a comfort.[12]

Could there be in us a chasm of fears, doubts or loneliness? Joy! Joy of the soul! The depths of anxiety in us call out to other depths – the inexhaustible compassion of his love.[13]

And to our surprise: trust was at hand, and so often we were unaware of it.[14]

Jesus, the Christ, never abandons us to the anguish of a solitude where all that remains is greyness, morose-ness and sadness.

[12] Jesus told his disciples that when he left them the Holy Spirit would be their comfort and their support (John 14.16–18; 26–27). 'God is called the "God of consolation", the "God of mercies", because his constant concern is to comfort, to encourage the unfortunate and the afflicted, even if they have committed thousands of sins.' (Saint John Chrysostom, fourth century)

[13] 'Deep calls to deep' (Psalm 42.7). When some people experience a kind of inner void, they come to the point of asking themselves: 'but where is God?' We may doubt, but God does not love us any the less for that. Does not the risen Christ remain alongside every person, even those who do not know him? Some Christians are utterly disconcerted when they are told that their faith is merely the projection of unconsciously infantile attitude. Doubt can then creep into their souls. But doubt is not always fearsome. The maturity of an inner life enables us to discover a way forward from doubt and hesitation to a humble trusting in God.

[14] When it comes to trusting in God, it is good that we hold on to a few Gospel truths and return to them constantly: 'In all things peace of heart, joy, simplicity, mercy.' 'In Christ forget what assails the heart.' 'God buries our past in the heart of Christ and is going to take care of our future.'

Ever since he rose from the dead, his presence has been made tangible through a mystical and visible communion, that communion of love which is the Body of Christ, his Church.

Finding fulfillment in this communion requires a simplicity of heart and of life. Without such simplicity, how can we go forward trusting in Christ?

Is the Church not entering a period today when it is being stripped to the essentials? Its credibility is at stake. This is all the more the case since in some parts of the world people are moving away from the faith.

Trust in Christ is not conveyed by means of arguments which attempt to persuade at all costs and so end up causing anxiety and even fear.

Amongst the younger generations, some remain at a distance from that communion which is the Church.

The question arises: 'Could they too be victims of age-old and brand-new divisions?'

Is it not urgent today to be reconciled by love? And when Christ calls, who can refuse? Who can forget his words: 'Be reconciled without delay?'[15]

---

[15] Matthew 5.23–24. Is hope for a reconciliation among Christians vanishing, like a wave that falls back? Perhaps, but does not God always open up new ways? Reconciliation is born from within, in the heart of each person, in their own life. The ecumenical vocation of the baptized is above all to be creators of a reconciliation that is made concrete each day, both near and afar. Lived out within one's own being, reconciliation acquires a credibility and can lead to a reconciliation in that communion of love which is the Church. What matters is to live as people who are reconciled. Documents will come later. Does not devoting too much energy to documents take us away in the end from putting into practice concretely the Gospel call: to be reconciled without delay?

Will we have hearts large enough, imaginations open enough, love burning enough to enter upon that Gospel way: to live as people who are reconciled, without delaying a single day?[16]

When the Church listens, heals, reconciles, it becomes what it is at its most luminous – the limpid reflection of a love, and still more, an abyss of consolation.[17]

Never distant, never on the defensive, freed from all forms of severity, the Church can let the humble trusting of faith shine right into our human hearts.

---

[16] There are countless Christians who undergo an inner struggle and often suffering in their attempt to be bearers of peace in that communion of love which is the Body of Christ, his Church. They are not naive when confronted with abuses that corrode communion. They could criticize the inflexible attitudes of some people. Far from allowing themselves to be drawn in that direction, they strive for silence and love with all their soul. When they express their desires, they are careful not to dig ditches which could separate people still more. They search for all that stimulates us to live as people who are already reconciled. They know that, with a view to the continuities of Christ in the human family, it is so essential for there to appear the reality of a communion, of a Church that is reconciled, where joy, simplicity and mercy dwell.

[17] Because of the separation between Christians, some find themselves in a situation where they cannot receive the Eucharist. Rather than becoming upset over this difficulty, it is possible to offer 'blessed bread' to everyone present at the celebration of the Eucharist, to all without exception, both believers and non-believers. This sign of hospitality is rooted in the story of the multiplication of the loaves. One day Christ blessed five loaves of bread and distributed them to all without distinction (Matthew 14.13–21). This leads us to reflect on the Church's motherly love; because of it she has managed to discover the unexpected. Does not this gesture, brought into being long ago among Eastern Christians, offer a concrete response in certain situations today?

Simplicity of life

A Gospel light, however feeble it may be, pierces our darkness with its rays.[18] It is fire; it is Spirit. It enables us to live Christ's life both within ourselves and for others.

In this period of history, there is an unprecedented awakening of the Christian conscience with regard to human suffering.

Everywhere in the world, there are Christians who are giving their lives. They are trying to be present amidst the increasingly rapid evolutions of society. In the midst of such rapid changes, a wonder arises; wonder at all that is made possible by love. Wherever they live, these Christians take on responsibilities that are often very specific.[19]

In vast regions of the world, human beings are measured above all in economic terms, and the desire to get rich through the market becomes an overriding obsession.

The consciences of a great many Christians cannot be satisfied by an economic growth that benefits only part of a country's population.

---

[18] 'God is light; in him there is no darkness.' (I John 1,5)

[19] Among Christians, there are many who refuse to accept any form of exclusion for others: unemployment, underprivilege in areas of large cities . . . There are young people, as well as not-so-young and elderly persons, who devote part of their time to volunteer service for others, for example by spending time with children or old people in their neighbourhood. Some support this volunteer work by collecting funds, and this is fine. But it is desirable that young people accomplish such service without any appeal for funds: three or four people can help others by sharing their meagre resources.

20

From the time of the apostles, the Virgin Mary and the first believers, there has been a call towards a simplicity of life.

One of the pure joys of the Gospel is to go further and further toward a simplicity of heart that leads to a simplicity of life.

Attentive to building up the human family, how can we remain unaware that every people has its own genius?[20] And so many peoples on earth today reflect the mysterious figure of the suffering servant:[21] humiliated, ill-treated, with nothing to attract us, it is our diseases that they bear.[22]

[20] We are in a period when a crisis of confidence in man is widespread. Particularly noticeable in Europe, it sets before us this challenge: what responsibilities can we take on so that a new confidence can be born, utterly indispensable for the building up of Europe?

[21] See Isaiah 53.2–4,7.

[22] Happy are those who have done all they could in recent years to bring about the freedom of their peoples! Who will uphold these freedoms in places where they are still quite new?

Let us not quench the fire!

At whatever point we may be, the risen Christ searches tirelessly for us and he always comes to us. Let us ensure we hear him knocking at our door and telling us: 'Come, follow me!'[23]

He desires that, with almost nothing, both fire and Spirit be made perceptible in us, above all through the gift of our lives.[24]

However poor we may be, let us not quench the fire. Let us not quench the Spirit.[25] In them are kindled the wonder of a love.

And the humble trusting of faith is communicated from one person to the next, like a fire that spreads.

[23] See Revelation 3.20 and Mark 10.21. Going to the very extreme of the gift of ourselves by a yes for an entire lifetime can be a support for those who take to heart the continuities of Christ. This yes is an anchor for inner freedom and the reminder of a clear meaning of life in the Gospel: to give it for others. They are truly present throughout the world, those who, by the gift of themselves, reflect something of the holiness of Christ without even realizing it.

[24] John the Baptist announced that Christ would baptize 'in the Holy Spirit and in fire'. (Matthew 3.11)

[25] I Thessalonians 5.19.

Photos:

Cover, pp.5,17,23: Taizé Community;
p.9: Sabine Leutenegger; pp.12/13: Vladimir
Sichov.

Published in Great Britain by
Geoffrey Chapman/Mowbray
A Cassell imprint
Wellington House, 125 Strand, London WC2R 0BB

Published in North America by
Westminster/John Knox Press
100 Witherspoon Street, Kentucky 40202–1396, USA

© Ateliers et Presses de Taizé 1996

Originally published in 1995 as *Étonnement d'un
amour*, © Ateliers et Presses de Taizé
F–71250 Taizé Community, France.

English Translation © Ateliers et Presses de Taizé
1995.

English language edition first published in The
Letter from Taizé 1995

British Library Cataloguing-in-Publication Data
A catalogue record for this book is available from
the British Library.
ISBN
0–264–67417–0 (Geoffrey Chapman Mowbray)
0–664–25685–6 (Westminster/John Knox Press)

Typeset by Keystroke, Jacaranda Lodge,
Wolverhampton
Printed and bound in Germany

For details of other Taizé books, recordings and
videos, please contact Cassell in the UK and
Westminster/John Knox Press in North America
or Taizé itself, at the addresses given on this page.